The Earth

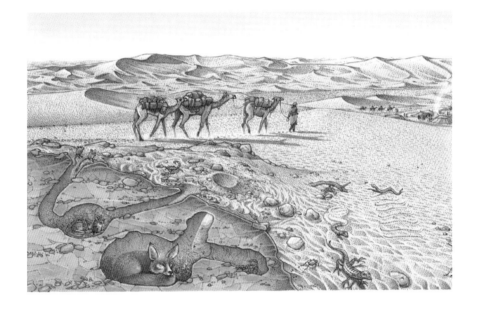

Angela Royston

Illustrated by
Jonathan Adams

Contents

First published in Great Britain in 1997 by Heinemann Children's Reference,
an imprint of Heinemann Educational Publishers, Halley Court, Jordan Hill, Oxford, OX2 8EJ,
a division of Reed Educational & Professional Publishing Ltd.

MADRID ATHENS PRAGUE WARSAW FLORENCE PORTSMOUTH NH
CHICAGO SAO PAULO SINGAPORE TOKYO MEXICO MELBOURNE
AUCKLAND IBADAN GABORONE JOHANNESBURG KAMPALA NAIROBI

© Reed Educational & Professional Publishing Ltd, 1997

ISBN 0 431 06547 0

British Library Cataloguing in Publication Data
Royston, Angela, First look through earth
1. Earth - Juvenile literature 2. Climatology - Juvenile literature
I. Title II. Earth 550

Photo credits: page 6: ZEFA-Pacific Stock © Reggie David; page 7: Tony Stone Worldwide © Chris Harvey; page 8: Bruce Coleman
Limited © 1993 John Cancalosi; pages 9 and 17: ZEFA; page 10: Britstock-IFA © Eric Bach; page 16: Tony Stone Images ©
Lori Adamski Peek, page 18: © David Hiser, and page 21: © Sally Mayman; page 23: Bruce Coleman © M P L Fogden.

Editor: Alyson Jones
Designer: Nick Avery
Picture Researcher: Liz Eddison
Art Director: Cathy Tincknell
Production Controller: Lorraine Stebbing

Printed and bound in Italy.
See-through pages printed by SMIC, France.

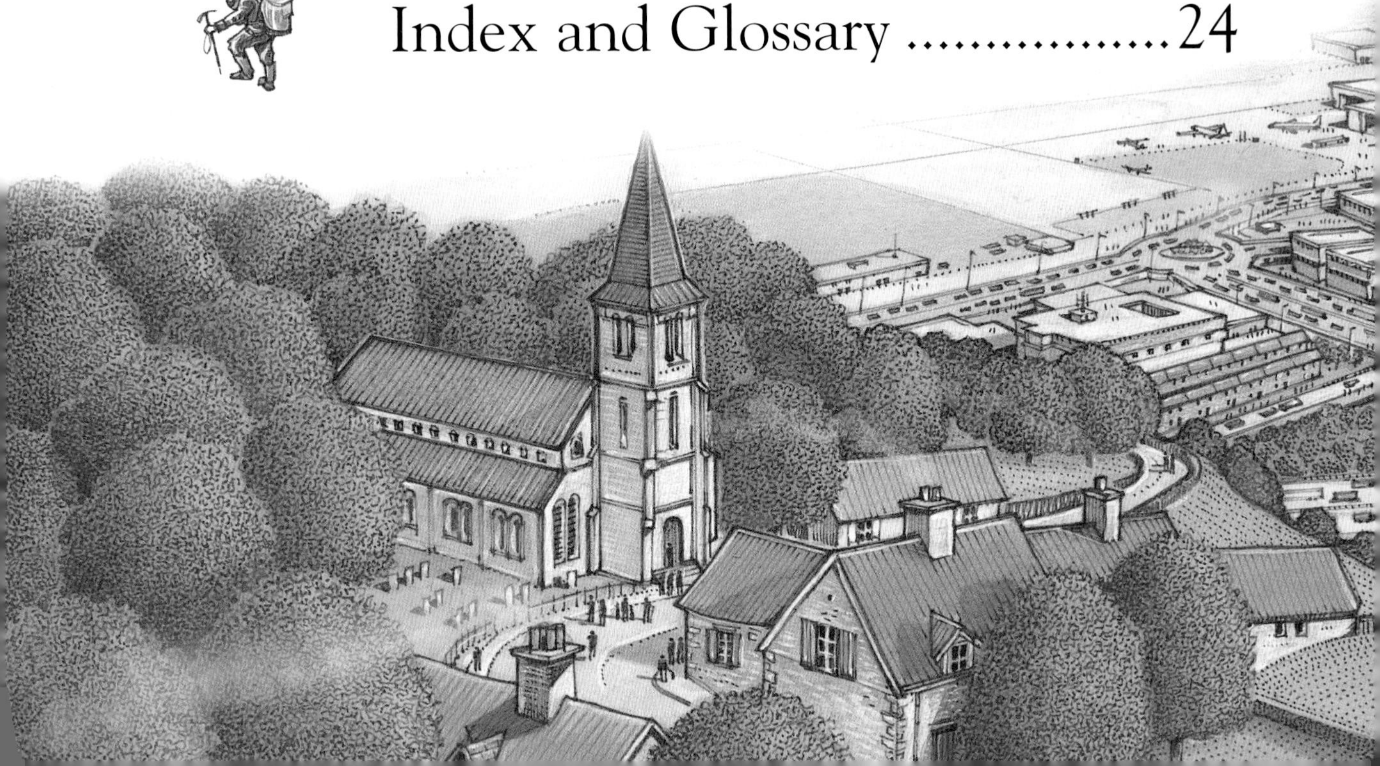

Our Earth

The Earth is a huge, round ball that spins through space. This is what the Earth looks like from a spacecraft. Can you see the land, the oceans and the clouds?

A map shows you what the Earth would look like if you could make it flat. There are seven continents. Where do you live?

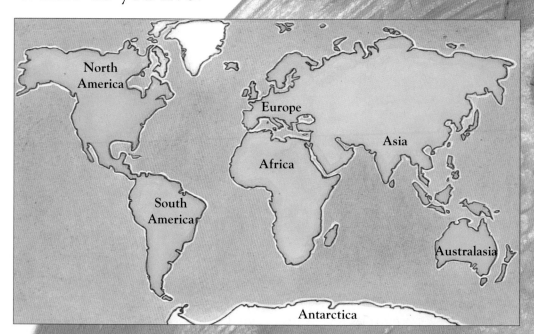

North America

Europe

Asia

Africa

South America

Australasia

Antarctica

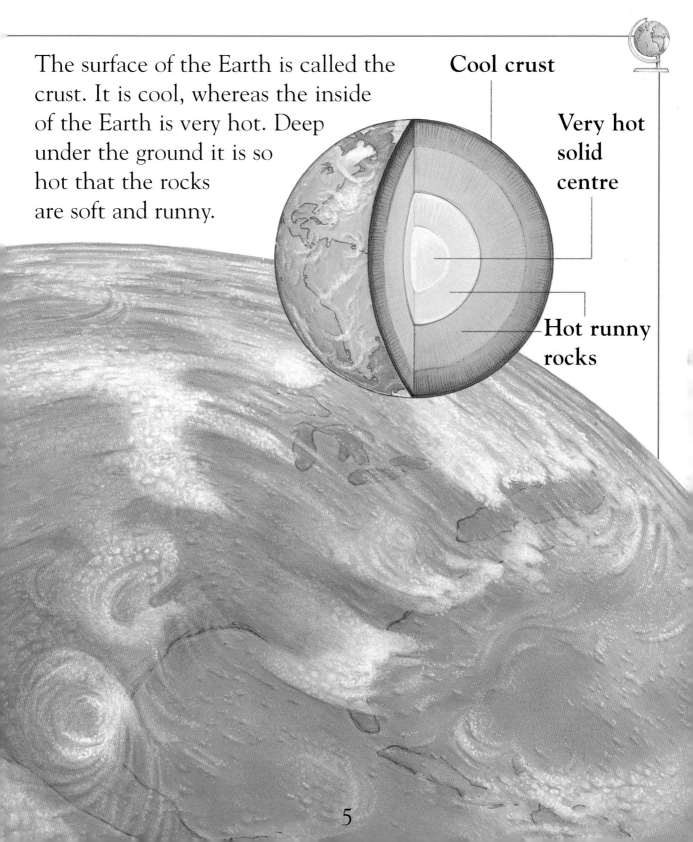

The surface of the Earth is called the crust. It is cool, whereas the inside of the Earth is very hot. Deep under the ground it is so hot that the rocks are soft and runny.

Cool crust

Very hot solid centre

Hot runny rocks

High and Low

Some of the land on the Earth is low and flat, but in other places it forms high mountains and deep valleys. Most mountain tops are snowy. Some people like to climb them. Others go up on a chairlift and then ski down.

This volcano in Hawaii is erupting! Red-hot lava from inside the Earth flows down the mountain. Many mountains were once volcanoes.

Flat grasslands stretch for hundreds of kilometres across the plains of Africa. Many birds and wild animals, such as these gentle antelope, live there.

Under the Ground

There are amazing things beneath the ground. People drill deep into the Earth's crust to look for precious stones, metals, coal and oil.

Coal and oil are found in some layers of rock. Miners travel deep underground to dig the coal.

This huge ruby has been dug from the ground. It will be cut into smaller stones and polished.

Power stations burn oil and coal to make electricity. Without electricity there would be no lights or television!

Pot-holers like to explore underground caves. Where are these people going?

Many animals dig homes in the soil. This rabbit cares for her babies in the burrow.

 # The Land

People have used the land on Earth in many ways. At one time it was covered in fields and forests. Farmers grew crops and kept animals in the fields. Now, most of the trees have been cut down and people have built cities on the land.

Roads criss-cross over the countryside. People need roads to travel from place to place, but too many roads can spoil the countryside.

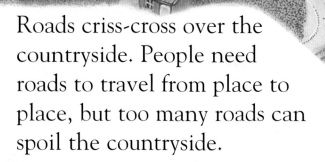

Drop your empty bottles in the bottle bank. They will be crushed and made into new ones. Glass, metal cans and paper can all be recycled.

Earthquake!

Sometimes the solid ground beneath our feet shakes and trembles. Usually we hardly notice, but in some parts of the world the shaking can be very violent. The ground cracks and the buildings sway.

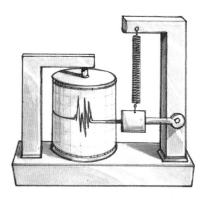

Scientists use special instruments, like this, to measure how strong an earthquake is.

Sometimes an earthquake under the sea makes a huge wave called a tsunami. When the wave hits the shore, it smashes boats and floods towns all along the coast.

Only a few buildings are left standing. They were built in a special way to make them safe, even in an earthquake. What has happened to the road?

Rainwater

When rain falls from the clouds onto high mountains, it freezes into ice. As the ice melts, the water runs down the mountains and into small streams. These streams join up to make a river. Where does the river go?

Rain puddles soon dry up as the water goes back into the air to form clouds. The wind blows the clouds and the rain falls again somewhere else.

Rain fills lakes and reservoirs.
Some of the water is carried in
pipes to our homes. People
can also sail on the reservoir.

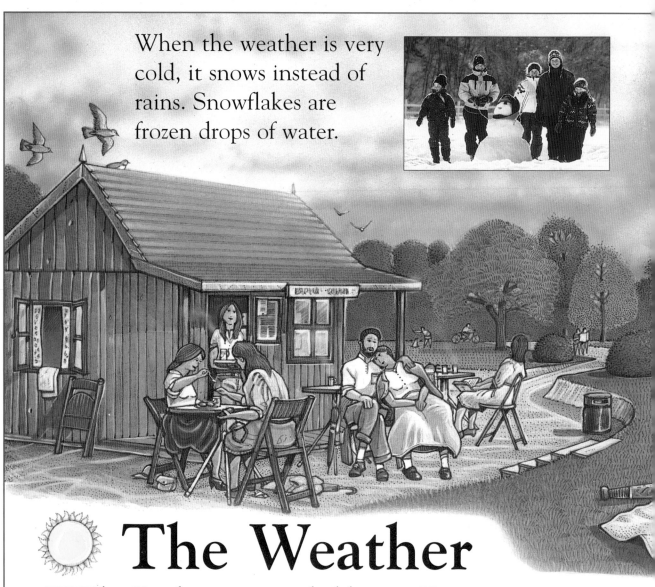

When the weather is very cold, it snows instead of rains. Snowflakes are frozen drops of water.

The Weather

The Earth is surrounded by air. You cannot see the air, but you can feel it when the wind blows. It is fun to have a picnic on a warm sunny day, but can you see the dark clouds coming? They are made of tiny droplets of water.

When the clouds cannot carry any more water, the water falls as rain. Then people run for shelter! Who do you think will get the wettest?

Thunder storms can be very frightening. The lightning flashes through the sky towards the ground. A rumble of thunder follows each flash of lightning.

Oceans

More than half of the Earth is covered by water. Fish and other animals live in the oceans. The boat is catching fish for people to eat.

There are even mountains under the sea! Some of them are so high the tops appear above the water to form islands.

Can you see the holes in these cliffs? They are made by the sea wearing away the rocks. Waves crash against the coast and change the shape of the land.

Deserts

It hardly ever rains in the desert. Very few plants grow there because they need water to survive. Many animals in the desert live under the ground because it is so hot.

Desert wind blows sand into dunes. These look like huge waves in the desert. Some deserts are rocky and stony, instead of sandy.

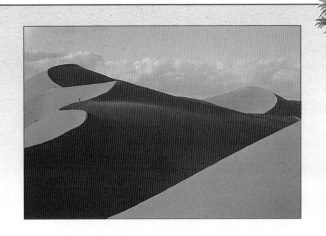

Travellers head towards the oasis. This is one of the few places in the desert where there is water. The camels will get a drink there!

Rainforests

Some parts of the world get lots of rain. Plants grow easily there. They can grow so thick and tall they form huge rainforests. Many animals live there, too. Can you spot the snake and the crocodile?

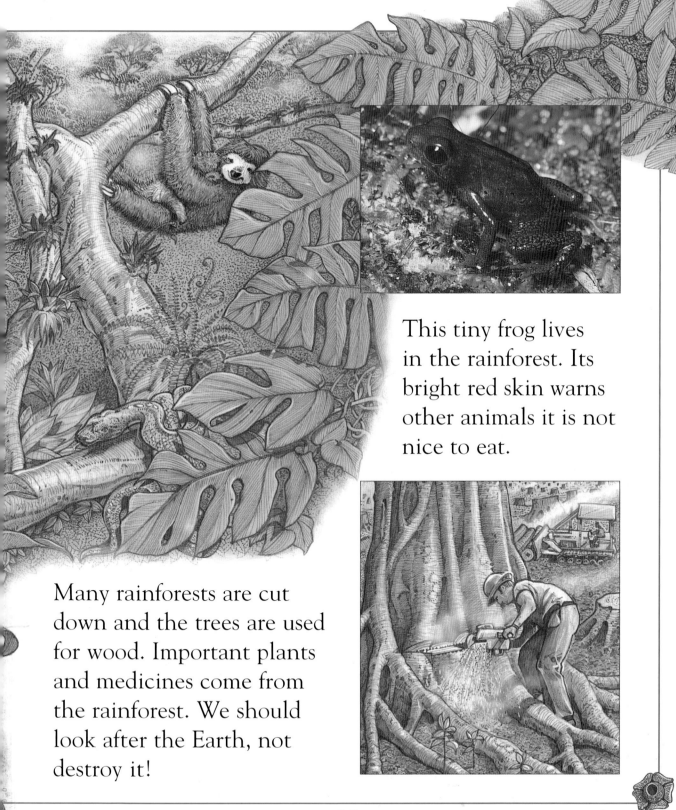

This tiny frog lives in the rainforest. Its bright red skin warns other animals it is not nice to eat.

Many rainforests are cut down and the trees are used for wood. Important plants and medicines come from the rainforest. We should look after the Earth, not destroy it!

Index

Glossary

Continent	a huge area of land	**Recycling**	reusing glass, paper or metal to make new things
Crops	plants grown for food		
Crust	a hard outer surface		
Dune	a hill of sand	**Reservoir**	a large lake for storing water
Electricity	energy that can be changed into heat and light		
		Ruby	a red precious stone
Island	land surrounded by sea	**Thunder**	a loud noise heard after a lightning flash
Lava	hot, runny rock from below the Earth's crust. It erupts from volcanoes		
		Volcano	a weak place in the Earth's crust where hot, runny rocks burst through
Oasis	a place in the desert where there are plants and water